Only What's Imagined

Also by Geof Hewitt

POETRY

I Think They'll Lay My Egg Tomorrow

Just Worlds

Living in Whales: Vermont Public School Stories & Poems (ed.)

Poem & Other Poems

Quickly Aging Here: Some Poets of the 1970's (ed.)

Selected Poems of Alfred Starr Hamilton (ed.)

Stone Soup

Today You Are My Favorite Poet: Writing Poems with Teenagers

Writing Without Walls: Boise Writing in the Schools
    (ed. with James Hepworth)

POEMS IN PERFORMANCE

The Maple Corner Tape: Poems from Vermont
    (with Chuck Meese)

NONFICTION

A Portfolio Primer

Today You Are My Favorite Poet: Writing Poems with Teenagers

Working for Yourself

Only What's Imagined

Geof Hewitt

THE KUMQUAT PRESS
Calais, Vermont

ACKNOWLEDGMENTS

The author wishes to thank the editors of the following publications, where some of these poems first appeared: Big Fish, Cedar Rock Review, The Colorado Review, Cornell Alumni News, Exquisite Corpse, The Green Mountains Review, Harpers, New Letters, The Paris Review, Poetry Now, and Potato Hill Poetry.

"Stone Gathering" first appeared in *The Corn*, a chapbook published by The Blue Moon Press.

"R.I.P. Rap," "Black Hole," "Dabbling in Oils," and "The Last Words" were first published in *I Think They'll Lay My Egg Tomorrow*: Vermont Council on the Arts/Steinhour Press.

The author gratefully acknowledges the Vermont Arts Council for its generous support of this publication.

Published by THE KUMQUAT PRESS,
            P.O. Box 51, Calais, VT 05648.

First Edition
Designer: Maureen O'Connor Burgess
Cover Photograph: Janet Lind Hewitt

Publisher's Cataloguing in Publication Data
811.54
H   Hewitt, Geof, 1943-
            Only what's imagined/poems by
        Geof Hewitt. Introduction by
        Hayden Carruth. — Calais, VT:
        The Kumquat Press, (c) 2000
        74 pages
        I. Title

ISBN 0-9676787-0-6

THE KUMQUAT PRESS
P.O. Box 51
Calais, Vermont 05648

Only What's Imagined

Three

INTRODUCTION

Poems, poems, poems – it seemed as if they were sprouting from the trees, even in dead of winter, and I do mean dead. Sometimes in January it was so cold and quiet you could hear Wallace Stevens thinking up a new poem down there in Connetchicutty. Well, we had a lovely forest. Kinnell in Sheffield, Engels in Williston, Voigt and Gluck in Plainfield, Budbill in Wolcott, Broughton and Huddle in Burlington, Rich in West Barnet, myself in Johnson, and – happily – Hewitt in Enosburg and Calais. A peculiar forest, no doubt; every tree was different, a species unto its own. No conformity. Maybe that's why we had such good times together and never suffered any territorial competition.

Truly, it was the finest literary society I've ever lived in, and I miss it terribly in my enforced exile in upstate New York. Circumstances, since 1980, have kept me from living in Vermont, which I still think of as home.

Geof Hewitt was our cut-up, the one who made us laugh the most, and we laughed a lot. His mind was like a squirrel scolding us from every branch. I've never known anyone so inventive, so full of good-natured rage, so antic in his refractoriness, and yet so gentle. He could puncture our sentimentality and leave our sentiment intact.

> It's delicate when we touch
> each other, a careful mistake
> will do but nothing more.

His wit, inexhaustible, was always acute but forbearing. Clement is not a word we use much now, but it's the word for Hewitt. He was and is the good friend of us all, and his poems were and are our delight.

But let me say a few sober and earnest words about our origin.

1

Like other rural areas, northern Vermont has generated a strange cultural mix in recent decades. When Geof Hewitt arrived in the late 1960s, coming from New Jersey by way of Cornell and Johns Hopkins, he found a poor agricultural society fundamentally unchanged since the eighteenth century. But Hewitt was part of a large immigration of outsiders, many of them young and idealistic, who sought escape from the crassness of mainstream America, and who admired the local inhabitants and became friends with them and absorbed much of their lore and manners. Life based on an alliance with nature amidst the hardships of the north appealed to them. At the same time, however, these newcomers retained their idealism, their devotion to rock music and social protest, their independence from convention. The result was that the newcomers changed Vermont as much as Vermont changed them.

No better poetic record of this cross-cultural amalgamation could be found than in the writing of Geof Hewitt. He bought a dilapidated farm in Enosburg, the region known as Cold Hollow, and soon afterward he and Janet Lind, who was from Iowa and had lived in Colorado, were married. They came to call on me one summer day and brought me a jug of somewhat-hard cider. We sat under my maple by the woodshed and drank it and talked. Geof was a young poet who had printed a poem of mine in his little magazine, *Kumquat*. He had founded the Kumquat Press in 1966 to publish *Poem & Other Poems*, a pamphlet of his own work, and had then expanded the enterprise to include his magazine and occasional pamphlets by other poets. Janet, born and raised on a farm in southeastern Iowa, was essentially a farmer, i.e., a farmer-without-a-farm, since the place in Enosburg would have needed an enormous investment of funds to make it workable. Our friendship was immediate.

Before long Janet took a job milking cows on a neighboring farm in Enosburg. Geof worked as a free-lance writer, did odd jobs, wrote poetry, and was a poet-in-the-schools with the state arts council. After a while they moved from the farmhouse into a cabin they built with the help of friends, at the edge of the woods overlooking Cold Hollow. It was a sturdy, two-story cabin, but "unimproved," as they say – no electricity, no plumbing. It was one of the coziest, most enjoyable abodes I've ever known.

Some years later Janet and Geof moved to Calais, to the section called Maple Corner. Janet became a librarian and teacher in the public schools. Geof worked in Montpelier, first with the Vermont Arts Council and then with the state education department, where he still is. In other words the reality of financial need overtook them. Geof continued to write, he published several books, he gave readings. He continued his association with the other poets of Vermont, most of whom had come at about the same time he did and for the same reasons. He became something of an impresario, arranging public readings and concerts throughout the state. He lectured in libraries and galleries. He directed workshops. He traveled widely to give readings and participate in literary conferences.

But make no mistake. Hewitt is a fully assimilated Vermonter, engaged unreservedly in the native life of the state, social, political, academic, and artistic, just as he is a fully committed poet who has been writing consistently, devotedly for more than thirty years. The history and heritage of Vermont are as important to him as to anyone. Likewise the history and heritage of poetry.

Probably no environment could have been better chosen for fostering Hewitt's special talents. He is a man of wit, even a jokester, in the best tradition of New England slyness and sardonicism. He

3

loves the outré and unlikely. Elsewhere he might be called an absurdist. He's an avid gardener, for instance, who grows California artichokes – with difficulty – as well as corn and potatoes, and pumpkins of exaggerated size. He is close to nature but delights in nature's improbabilities. At the same time he is an intelligent guy, obviously, a student of the social and political scene, a concerned husband and father. Above all he is a man fascinated by language.

His influences? Well, surely Frost. We all must admit to that. But also David Ray, Edward Field, A. R. Ammons, David Budbill, Donald Hall and, he says, myself. (When a poet has read enough of a friend's work, probably that voice kicks in from time to time, whether wanted or not.) His poems are tough, very original, occasionally sentimental, usually keen and caustic. His language is knotty, sometimes abrupt and anti-syntactical, but never cryptic. His topics are unconfined, anything that happens. His poems, properly read, are a better reflection of his time and place than any sociological dissertation could ever be.

I'm tempted to call this poetry, retrospectively, Neo-Classical or even Late Metaphysical, not a fashionable kind of poetry in our time. Yet for my part I can draw a straight line from Andrew Marvel to Geof Hewitt, and the line is perfectly secure at both ends in spite of the distance between them. This is a mode, a sensibility, in which I have always taken delight – the fusion of natural observation and metaphysical awareness in vivacious, trenchant, witty poems. No whispering or mumbling, as we find in so much poetry nowadays. Hewitt is far too confident of his own imagination to suppress it, and justly so. In short these are very fine poems. I recommend them heartily to everyone.

Hayden Carruth

One

MISSING THE PROOF

In my own little world
I rush against the passing season
and try to get a start on the season coming:
winter cut wood for next winter;
springtime get the tiller going
haul manure and fence the garden right this time;
summer pull weeds and build a chicken coop;
fall stack wood and cut wood that didn't get cut last winter.

The sun inches lower in the sky each day,
and starts back up before winter is even half-started,
season after season, eventually so far behind
winter finds me cutting wood one day to burn the next until
I build a fire to warm me in the woods
and burn what I cut so there's nothing to haul home
and in panic my family searches my flushed face
demanding me to prove I worked all day.

My young daughter sniffs where her nose reaches my belly
and remarks I smell like cutting wood
while my older son and wife look me in the eye
for a trace of lost confidence.
They have huddled at the stove all day waiting.
Perhaps tomorrow they will be cold enough to help,
but for the night we sleep in the same bed
under heaps of blankets pooled from our rooms.

I dream of my own importance in life
until by some breach of common sense
I feel that I have been the constant
and the sun an incidental body on the run.

THE DAMP OCTOBER

leaves fell in clumps
and browned before their brighter colors

could hold

I remember well the mud tracks
dragged across the floor,
dried to heavy dust by noon & swept out the door
puffing I shall return

bum's rush
we always think we got our dirt by the scruff

how we treat the heart
how we use soil as a verb

UPSIDE DOWN

Upside down, my pants hang from the line
Depending from a pair of wooden clothespins
One to each leg. The waist is three inches too high
To scuff the leaves, though six weeks from now
We'll have to raise the line or double
The trousers over at the thighs to keep the waist
From dragging snow. Come a good January thaw
We could hang a pair by the cuffs and let the waist freeze
Into the puddle where melted snow froze fast
At the snap end to the thaw, then
Unpin the cuffs and remove the line so a flat pair of pants
Is stiff and vertical upside down executive
Who plunged head first into the earth, up to his waist!

SPECTRUM

Excited by the clearness of the night,
the quarter moon's smile
in a sky full of stars,

we remarked, almost colorful,
our three shadows on the snow.
It's the moon, she said,

that makes those images
but without the stars you'd never get the blues.

A giant timber in the forest cracked.
No matter.
The child was talking.

Where was I going?
Was I going home forever
or would I return to the walk?

I'm going back to write a poem,
I replied, I'll never return.
That was good enough for them.

They headed down the path
with their black and blue shadows.

THIS IS GROSS

but I cough up a good one
and whistle-thrust it through my lips
into the blazing furnace fire
where it catches halfway up a maple chunk
and sleazes into a giant teardrop
before starting to sizzle.

This is gross but it begins to puff up,
having sealed and trapped sufficient air
to expand it to the size and shape
of a giant cocoon: it seems to pop
but returns from half-inflated to its greatest girth
repeatedly, breathing like a heart confused.

At last I understand how fire might make the parts of life
and from the popping seed they issue, rudiments of speech.

IN LIKE A LION

The white howl of March
Sweeps down from Canada.
A glove is frozen to the spade.
The rope holds a defiant curve,

It smiles at gravity.
I stamp out your name in the snow
So big great altitude is needed to read.
And, "I am a lonely secret

Like pajamas stuffed with pillowcases."
How yesterday's sunshine made me feel
I'd got to spring scot-free,
How lovely to hear it come through branches

Through open window like a voice
You love says let's dance.

SYLLABLES

Though every generation claims its share of Frosts,
the only real or self-appointed Frost was Robert Frost himself.
Anyway, you need a name for an accolade? Mantel of syllables
or letters embossed on special license plates,
Look out! That big white Lincoln whooshed
past your wagon on the interstate.
If you could have kept up you'd have tailgated,
trusting inside the reflective glass rode a radar detector,
you could speed with impunity. Or perhaps it was a sting:
ambitious cop from Washington
ready to arrest you or a state trooper
off duty, driving home at dusk in an official car,
accepts bribe in the twilight
and winds up in the slammer for a year.

Vermont's got its prisons but when a man from Florida,
visiting his second summer in a row,
learned we have six "correctional" facilities
for adult law-breakers, his mouth dropped.
He'd been upset the week before to hear
Frost wasn't born in Vermont, but this time
he nearly cried. I could have mentioned other institutions.
He wasn't so interested that inmates need contact
with the world's ideas and people as by the fact
that in St. Albans and St. Johnsbury, in Burlington
and Windsor, Rutland and Woodstock
are jails. I changed the subject and he relaxed
enough I got my point across
about the book we were discussing.

The prison with the nicest coordinator
had the loudest iron doors,
visitors constantly reminded
what inmates take for granted
as a fetus adjusts to its mother's breathing
or miners adapt to conditions that kill them.
David Budbill's poems were the subject.
The cultural coordinator said she often found
his book's Vermonters "stick figures — personality types."
A young inmate from Tennessee:
"If so it's because Vermonters
didn't let the author close enough to them."
These syllables from one with three more years
in a place some people don't know exists.

Another participant expressed contempt:
"That writer's got it made. Play was produced here in town."
But when the poems passed his expectations,
they touched him with familiar syllables,
arranged in another version of the truth: he liked the book.
The people of Vermont are not just the Yankee farmers,
whose "industry" crumbled in twenty years,
with 2,739 of 5,264 dairy farms gone since 1969.
The growth in tourism eased the sting
and like as not farmers
from the 70's tend ski lifts and bars
on gorgeous mountain tops or drive trucks
or work at the university or in state government
or sell hardware, teach school, edit, chair committees

while 2,500 still hay the fields and milk cows
for which Vermont is famous. As malls and shopping centers
replace the dairy herds and crops, what's a man to do?
Frost would have captured it with irony
and maybe played a hand in helping to reverse
a stone's fate in quicksand, nearly my fate once
when marching through a neighbor's barnyard to collect
on a debt, I got two feet
into the manure pit and sinking fast
finally figured to reverse direction.
My neighbor never said, when I asked for the check,
"We'd never have missed you," though he could tell
from the level of things in the air,
and on my trousers, where I'd been.

The people of Vermont? You'll know them
one or two at a time, not through annual Town Meetings
or around a single ritual like sugaring or potluck dinners,
and they'll fool you. You've got to be persistent,
a journalist, unless you've got a lifetime.
So when I asked Hugh Gross "How was sugaring this year?"
he said "Not bad." I rephrased the question, knowing it
had been a banner year. "Best season ever?"
"Yup."
　　　　You'll know them one or two at a time,
and they'll fool you. When I arrived in '68,
I admired a house painter whose Yankee savvy
and accent obscured that he had lived
all but the past six years in New Jersey,
my home too. The cussedest Yankees
are the ones who got here late and have
to make up time like the Happy Trails Lady

15

never smiling except in the woods
or the woman from Scotland who won't look humans in the eye
unless she's about to let them take a pet
from her pound. She hates people for the abuse
she sees animals suffer. The next cussedest Yankees
are the Yankees themselves: take Harold, the farmer
whose old house and fields I bought when he quit farming
at sixty-five to drive the town tractor, maintain town roads, grading
and cutting brush. One summer day I was barefoot,
shirtless in shorts when he stopped to visit, yelling down
over the hot diesel engine, his blade
in thick roadside grass inches short

of a large rock. When we'd done talking
I sweated that rock, as he watched, from his path: I squatted
and worked it up, over bare toes, behind the cutter bar.
He smiled, touched his cap, lurched into gear and drove
up the road.
     The backstrap of his cap
winked in the bright afternoon as I saw the cutter bar raise
from its grass-height position
over some new roadside obstacle.

I built a chimney for the oil furnace I'd installed to replace Harold's
kerosene space heater. I never was told to mix sand with the mortar,
so the chimney blocks, hefted up a ladder leaned to the side of the
third story and braced by an ancient house, were never really leveled.
The final result had shape in common with a tall letter "S." Wendell
Savage, who grew up in the house before Harold bought it, saw the
chimney, smiled and scratched his chin, "I never saw smoke that
wouldn't bend." This phrase ever since has lessened my shame at
not reading details in the how-to books.

This morning I woke to thoughts of Patricia
and what's happened to her mother?
who used to walk her forty-year-old Patricia
through Montpelier and take her to the fairs
and big art openings, always in a matching yellow outfit,
Patricia equally bright in red or shocking pink.
When I was really awake I tended my face and dressed,
then saw Patricia on my way to work!
Her mother has probably died. "Dead as a flapped jack"
Patricia uttered in my morning dream,
the nearly waked state where a distant figure
becomes friend for life, someone you see
and care about, on the street in color if I dream in color,
the syllable or building block of lasting vision.

No death will keep Patricia at her mother's heel.
She walks Elm Street and goes in muted colors
to the fairs with a bigger smile
than ever. We're both out on the streets
and glad to live where we're needed.
Where notice of the mountains seems important,
where, after frost, leaves brown and scramble from the trees —
each a syllable in a long, hard sentence:
Winter — things become clear.
                    On a good November day I can see
six miles when even yesterday the view for the leaves was just ten feet.
The seasons keep me going, keep me hoping I can count
or somehow keep up with my debt,
my interest on my debt,
to Patricia and all others with whom on this planet I move.

THE COUNTRY POET

I want a new image, something with dash
To grind my tongue in.
Something our kids will have to learn in school.
But *what?* I try how dry I feel some nights
After the wood stove's used up all the air, dry as
Doggie do, but that's no good, dry as dust,
Dry like powder in a box, dry as ash.
My lines are these big clunks like hard cement.
And the sun goes down on another day of literary jerking off.

I envy Stanley his hourly wage and the end of his day
Of working for other men. He comes home
& tells the family, "Soon we're going to buy a farm."
I think I'll hire out as the trusty hand!
What Heaven it'll be to *have* to get up & warm my hands
On steaming udders thirteen out of every fourteen days!
I know how fortunate I am. My brain
Is like a baked potato waiting to be peeled.
The white meat is useful & something damp.

Stanley, oh Stanley. How easily the snow
Drops through the winter & lowers the hemlock's boughs.

THE SANDMAN

So I was coming around the corner and the car ahead of me has stopped and I'm on sheer ice and my car starts to skid and there's this guy on the sidewalk with a shovel and just before my car crunches into the car ahead of me he throws a shovelful of sand under my rear tires and my car comes to a stop ten feet from disaster.

Half an hour later I'm at the Xerox machine with a job I've gotta have copied in time for the mail, which leaves in ten minutes, and the machine jams and I'm trying to get the paper out and something throws a spark and ignites the paper so smoke is starting to curl from the ink drum and I'm trying to figure whether I should run to the men's room for a handful of water when this guy appears with a shovel and throws a shovelful of sand into the machine's underbelly and the smoking stops.

WHY I HATE OVERCOATS

When Swifty,
That sad, old prick,
Made me go back
Because the coat rule was still in effect,
Even though it was sunny & warm,

I knew future freedom
Lay in my ability to take the cold.

STONE GATHERING
-for John Cote

These marks in stone, these pocks
were forced into its surface when some ancient rain
lost its juice to stopped momentum

and saved its shape, splatting by pure luck
into rock that hadn't hardened yet. Then the river played
its part to roll the stone, to smooth

and to protect the finished rock.
You say pick flat ones only
and the big are best, it means

less work. A snail falls off
the one I'm working from the streambed
given up its home, losing suction

gone back to the brook, perhaps to find
another stone. I heave the snail's ex-home
up onto the bank and sit on it

and there decide this rock of every century
in the house you built
will brace someone whose hand,

feeling the work, stopped where the notion struck:
it's shaped as much by heaven's gentle water
as by men who build it into walls.

THE MOTHER PHOEBE
-for Heather

She has her second brood ready to fly
if only they would — four of them
elbow to elbow, cheek by jowl,
in the tiny nest under an eave of our porch.
Last summer, home at dusk
I stood on a chair for a peek
and four or five baby phoebes took just that moment
to burst forever from the nest: they startled me!

She chirps from the porch roof
then visits a bean pole from which she flies
to take a bug on the wing back to the nest
and leaves immediately with the peeping
of three disappointed, unfed big babies behind
as the one that was most aggressive
tries to swallow the oversized chunk of bug whole,
bug-eyed himself, blinking unbelievably into the
six inches of red yarn she worked into the nest
three or four springs ago.

Every place she lands she glances back
hoping, I guess, one of her unfed chicks
has got the message and will follow.
She moves from the pine to the clothesline
whereupon she poops on my son's
favorite tee shirt, a punk tee shirt
upon which the wearing of birdshit might well, by his peers,
be considered the ultimate statement of punkdom to date.

She's pissed at me for trying to observe
their privacy. I'd hoped she might recognize
my growth from last summer's chair-peering behavior,
my lawn stool arranged
in shadow for glare-free vision,
at least twenty feet from the nest.
A beak full of bugs and she can still scold
from the bean pole, her tail flicking up and down,
trademark of the perching phoebe.

Now *he* shows up, just after I discover
it's the cat was scaring her and put it in
then take my shady place again with beer and notebook,
pen in hand: a tourist in the land of birds,
they should open a hamburger stand.

They relay meals to the nest
and in their absence I hear the whirring wings
of overcrowded baby phoebes like the revved propellers
of commuter planes at the start of the runway.
Later one of them throws the clutch to exit the nest,
hangs mid-air like a hummingbird near a screened window,
then follows the mother to a nearby maple where
it chirps and peeps after her
as she calls from a more-distant perch.

Returning to the nest I count the fuzzy heads:
four still remain!
The one that just flew must have been sitting on a sibling.
In two more hours I check again; the nest is empty.

FOR HAYDEN

The tourist, happy to be alive in a place like Vermont,
turns to the local stuck here twelve months a year
and says, "Where do *you* go to get away?"
Then corrects himself with a quick addition:
"Of course anyone lucky enough to *live* here
        doesn't need to get away!"
And that's the end of friendship there,
the loss of universal feeling
to a lie, in this case a patronizing one
because the local knows
that s.o.b. can choose
and he's here only three days a year!

The tourist moves closer to the barbwire fence
for a better view of the farmer
astride his tractor with the side-bar cutter
and the grass is falling in waves parallel
to the last row that was felled
while the squared-off stand remaining
gets surrounded smaller and smaller.
The cutter doesn't jam and the tourist
thinks that's the farmer's life and I shared it
for ten minutes while he squared
his field and made hay.
Meanwhile, farmer thinking:
that poor bastard got some time off from the city
and best he can do is watch me drive.
Thank God nothing's going wrong.

And fingers a dincher from the floor of his pack
as the tourist turns
back to the waiting family and automobile,
a family that never chose to cease
bickering and exit the car, but instead to sweat
and call periodically for him to drive them on.
The farmer on his tractor cannot watch them at all times
cornering the field, he cannot look back
          as they disappear, his vision
is the stop-frame picture of their positions
every time his tractor is headed straight down the row
toward their parking spot,
each time the father, now grown familiar with his foot on a strand,
gazes at him in the foreground, the carful of family
parked in the shade, exasperated,
behind. He makes another square,
a little farther from them as he hays
toward dead center of the field.
When the tractor straightens to the row
that lets him see the tourists
they are gone.

They were too far off to see the field sparrow's well-hidden eggs
crumble under the cutter-bar, and they would never recognize
the all-day, redundant, useless scold
of the field sparrow and her mate whose nesting grounds
and potential family have been unbelievably erased
          lined up in horizontal rows
          like grease stains on an earthen plate.

They left too soon to hear the cutter-bar clank
against another grass-hidden object
        this time not eggs, but stone,
and the ripping free of iron and the
        engine's overheated coughing to a stop
in gritty, diesel-wafting heat.
The scold is darting at the farmer as he tries to
coax the wounded cutter back on the bar.
Only a square of grass remains to be mowed
and the tractor's engine is rough to restart in this heat.
He gooses and coughs it back into action,
jumps free and checks the motion of the bar.
It works and back he climbs, too high
to see the minute dangers of his work,
too far from the retreating tourist
rehearsing for Monday's coffee break
as he describes to wife and children
what they sat through and never saw
anything there to start with.

CHICKENS

And aren't those baby chicks
creatures of my acquiescence
letting a particularly broody banty hen
have some eggs to set?

Now she acts as if they're completely her
creation, even the rooster has to sneak
blessings to his heirs, and I
get pecked for coming near.

Those chicks get down under her belly
and stay warm in that darkness,
sputtling over each other in morning
when I remove the raincoat

from their cage, the limits of their world
so far. I make their day begin
by letting sunlight in, and feed & water them.
They peek out from underneath

their banty's feathered underside and peep:
"Hey that's Him! I saw God's hand unveiling day!"
And I sit here, twelve hours later, August 26
8:30 p.m. Already the sun is down.

Yeah, winter's coming.
Darkness — God! — I hate to see it come.

LEAF PEEPERS

New Mercedes van
with Jersey plates,
stuffed with tourists
scowling at a conifer:

"Damn.
We got here too early!"

FALL

The color drains from the daisy
as when, turned upside down, the dress on the lady in the liquid
barrel of my father's trick pen
lost its color & she was naked in there,

tiny & unreachable, nothing to do but
turn the pen back rightside up
& write a word or two as she got dressed
or smash the pen carefully.

Come to think of it, I didn't see a bee all summer,
& maybe that's why the plants hardly fruited,
why I didn't get stung even once this summer,
& hardly saw the male at my hummingbird feeder —

no competition with those flying thumbtacks
for all the good that drips inside the beebalm.
Lawn chairs left out in the hope of one more day of sun
are holding an important conference, their arms flat out

& serious, & when I walk the garden deep in weeds,
tomato plants long ago choked out by jewelweed,
I see within all that green & orange a tiny red globe,
almost unreachable,

& return by stepping carefully in the swath
I made coming in & see,
smashed against the green mat of footprints,
the colors of a crop that failed.

THE WATER

The water was doing what water does best,
which is soak things.
Which is finding its own level.
Which is leading to growth — plant growth
and then rot, which is back to the thirsty soil.

The water was doing what water does best,
it was dripping from every surface,
it was dripping from my hair and from my nose,
fingertips and elbows and from the cuffs of soaked pants
through sox into shoes.

And the nasty November wind was doing what it does best,
which is to take thin blood and flesh
to the just short of numb stage, Christ the water,
without that wind, would have seemed almost *warm*.
I was cursing my luck, out of gas, two miles from home

on a deserted country road, I was walking!
At 6 p.m. I was leaning into the driven rain,
not seeing any humor through wet lashes,
but already savoring the telling later,
around the fire, attentive audience, cocoa steaming in clay mugs:

the wind was whipping bullets of water
against my helpless face, while river currents
forced me backwards nearly half the time.
But I sang in the gathering darkness,
sang and brought my soggy groceries home,

doing what I do best.

Two

BLOCKS

These painted, hardwood blocks for children
were my father's first children's blocks:
passed down through his two families they stopped with me,
his final child, conceived when he was 55.

They stayed in my room until my brother's wife
had a nephew. I was in college and couldn't
care less. They all fit nicely
in a wagon with wheels that squeak.

These blocks are back now my nephew's 15,
Ben helps Anna stack them, they topple
heavy, hard, hurtful. Too often I stub
my bare, cold toes on innocent playthings

and every night on my knees, as a child
because of mother, as father by necessity
one by one I search them out
and fit them nicely the first time.

PIGSKIN

Spiro with a long i
is our word for spiral,
something I could never throw
except by luck
until this year.

With small hands
as a boy I couldn't hold
the fat pigskin
and carried into adulthood
the habit of clutching fingers

that finally found a hold
with the introduction of the pennyweight
rubbery foam Nerf ball
to a game that had formerly
left me frustrated.

Proud that my fingers could grasp
defiance of gravity,
I held the Nerf for every throw
so hard that my son Ben, on catching it,
would claim I'd left imprints

in the foam. "Cratered like the moon"
he'd crow, returning my heave
with an effortless spiro, the ball
all smoothed by the time
it spun into my arms.

By some mistake I got smart
a couple weeks ago and threw
before my fingers clamped
and the ball went out
to everyone's amazement like a bullet.

Within a day or two
I'd discovered and practiced my mistake
and now my son and I toss perfect spiros
back and forth until my arm gives out
and the ball is bored without bruising

and wobbling through the sky, bouncing wide,
bobbling off the edge of the hill,
chased by Ben who screamed:
"Stop! Come back! Bad throw!"

ORSON

The neighborhood beagle, ignored by family,
hated by the neighbors, is a car runner,
garbage eater, chicken killer who is,
nevertheless, kind with children
and has always treated me with decency
even if he does chase my car.
Shot and wounded, rumor had him dead
but we saw him the next day,
about the time Reagan was shot.
The owners kept him on a chain for a while,
but by the time Reagan was back in the Oval Office,
Orson was back on the loose, raising hell
and none the wiser for his brush with death.

Today, a first real spring-like Sunday,
he sauntered down our lane. I called him
to make friends, then as he came and got petted
I wondered would he misunderstand my attentions
and return for other goodies, my chickens,
my car, my trash?

MOONLIGHT

The boss thinks
      I'm devoted to my family.
At home they say
      I'm married to my work.

PATH POEM

They say the daughter at birth has all the eggs
she'll ever produce: the path is set at your mother's birth
as other paths unfold like a lifeline
in the gradual, almost imperceptible unclenching fist of time.

Some of these paths will come to coincidence:
it might be the accident
of a flat tire that delays you just enough
to miss the train that would have run you over,

and driving home with your suitcase stop at a bar
to inspect the tire then decide to have one
and meet a brilliant executive
who takes you into her confidence and within the year

you're flying in a private jet, riding limousines
with faultless tires and tuxedoed drivers
who know the quickest route and where to drop you
to celebrate time saved by such smart travel.

At times you think *you're* controlling the path,
how else would anyone be so lucky
if they weren't just plain smart:
maybe a brilliant executive?

But you crave time so *you* can climb into the tuxedo
and take *yourself* for a spin in the limousine,
enduring the snooty stares at stoplights from people in normal cars
who think you're a lowly chauffeur sporting about in the boss's rig.

Or maybe coming home that night
your headlights catch the eyes of a cat working the roadside:
it panics, running a path
diagonal across the road, under your front tire.

At midnight there's no finding an owner,
no one to comfort and thus make yourself feel better,
the teary master in a nightshirt telling you between sobs,
"It was only a cat."

Arriving home you slump from the vehicle
and feel your way in the dark.
You know the path can swing in front of fortune or misery
or zag between the two a whole life.

That's why I keep my fingers crossed, it's a form of prayer.

THE KIND OF POETRY I WRITE

I told him I think poetry is the language
that shares experience, not what is beautiful,
and I don't think I can use "moon" in my poems.
Of course, explaining it in a poem is kind of creepy.

I'm delighted someone would read this far,
and I never believed he'd listen:
each word a new chance
not to abuse an old cliche,

not to construct self-conscious language,
not to be beautiful, not to confound,
not to take a risk, not to discover, share,
not to be mystical,

that was what I was not writing for these days!
And I was sure depressed about it all.
I told him I'd published in a magazine.
"Resting on your laurels, eh?" he said.

Yeah, resting on my laurels
and driving home what I took to be the moon
— a smudge of light above Montpelier —
glowed like the top of a smokestack

and I kept driving along and my poem said
I never saw it I never said it

THE SAILOR

In my movie the boat goes under
And he alone survives the night in the cold ocean,
Swimming he hopes in a shoreward direction.
Daylight and he's still afloat, pawing the water
And doesn't yet know he's only fifty feet from shore.
He goes under for what will be the last time
But only a few feet down scrapes bottom.
He's suddenly a changed man and half hops, half swims
The remaining distance, hauls himself waterlogged
Partway up the beach before collapsing into sleep.
As he dreams the tide comes in
And rolls him back to sea.

THE GOLDFISH

If, as the famous composer suggested,
A fish tank's glass were painted
With the G-clef and horizontal lines
Of a musical staff,

Goldfish would compose the song
With quarter and half notes,
Rests and hours of silence
Determined by their fits and starts.

The music would have a random quality
Perhaps, to human ears.
But how the fish would dance
And how the water sing!

MOTH

After you cut the lights tonight
all the moths will burst into tears
that haven't already singed their wings
on what they think is the marvelous sun,

those unconsolable little light worshippers
will beat their wings to powder night after night
until all that's left are miniscule coat hangers
like skeletons poking from their puffy moth bodies.

How does a moth know to love the light
or is it hatred, this unflagging devotion, an ill-concealed fury
that makes it dive toward the brightest
or the only lit bulb in the house?

So how does an all-white, all-male jury react
when you fall in love with a moth? This pet
you've cultivated, trained and seek to wed?
Will they show compassion and sanction the union

or separate you forever by pulling the plug on your freedom,
committing you for decades to a darkened, padded cell?
Or do you play it cool and encourage the moth to keep quiet,
be discrete, don't brag about your human lover?

Hide the candles! Whisk away all matches.
Fall in love with a moth and you got another moth to feed.

THE WIFE AGREES

The wife agrees to cut my hair.
She's the cheapest game in town
And it doesn't hurt too much
Except when she clips my ears.
I guess she doesn't like being called the wife.

The little woman says I'm getting cocky
And tells me from now on I need an appointment.
None of this springing it on her at the last moment
Before a poetry reading
Or the gathering of important committees,

Tugs at the forelock and shoves my head to the side,
Maintains that the shears are too dull,
And leaves a moth hole on the left side
About which I generously complain.
I guess she doesn't like being called the little woman.

But I'm not gonna stop my bitching
About looking like a half-peeled onion.
So she takes the scissors and chops a grocery bag in half.
"Put this on the left side of your head," she says.
"Then people can only see your better half."

LIQUIDS

Coffee wakes you from that sleep-bruised face,
fraggles your nerves
till they push you out into the day, into the twitch.

Rain and dandruff slush creep through your boots,
feet seep. By noon you're ready
to swallow a Pepsi, it sparkles your throat

and in the new sun your sweat bakes as mud turns to dust
on your face. By 5 the excuse to stop: the whistle
runs through your ears, cuts a string in your head.

You become friends with the guy next to you
and agree to stop for a drink. The beer drags the day's crust down,
coats a glistening path and

in the corner of your eye, like the last thought before sleep,
something glints.
It reminds you   something   you can't remember.

A woman with pale powdered breasts and spots on her neck
nurses a brandy alexander and you buy her one.
Your friend from work has excused himself

till morning. He's got family, kids,
and each of you would trade places.
He could love the pale powdered darkness

and the chance to get lushed now and then
and you'd drink all those quarts of nonfat milk
just to get close to his wife

THE RIGHT WORDS

-for Jim

When I was a kid
and something bad happened to a neighbor
I tried to stay away until things had blown over:
I didn't know what to say.

My grandfather cut his left thumb clean off
with a table saw. He was a carpenter
making someone a table. He drove himself
to the hospital twelve miles

holding his red hand out the window at red lights
so traffic would know to let him through.
I didn't want to see him, no matter
that I loved him, hell, that made it harder,

but he was in our driveway before I knew
he was even out of the hospital
and before I could hug him or hide
he told me his thumb-stump had grown a new nail.

"Wanna see?" Tongue frozen
I nodded and saw
he held to his turbaned thumb
a six-penny nail from his shop.

A friend at a fancy dinner
asked her three-year-old son
who had just, by accident, farted loudly,
"Johnny, what do you say?"

46

The guests had paused in their talk
to study their reflections in the consomme.
The astonished child replied:
"Thank you."

What *does* one say, what are the right words?
My friend just lost half his house to a fire.
I said: "You're so calm.
I'd be throwing a fit."

He replied in a way that comforted me:
"I've thrown it already."

R.I.P RAP

Having someone to love isn't all it's cracked up to be.
It's 51% inspiration and 49% worry.
The inspiration makes the worry worse
Because if you didn't have the former the latter
Would dry up and scab off
Leaving you raw for something new.

But fact or fate is I'm gifted
With these loves, these inspirational worries
And I fear with horror what I'd be without them.
Carving here my epitaph, Goodbye My Loves
And Gone To A Better World and

Ha Ha
You Sorry Bastards
Look Who Got Here First

POTTER

Your hands at the wheel
pull a fat lump of clay,
almost will it,
up to a vase.

You make the hole with your thumb
and guide the flaring rim
so it stays round
but gets thinner and thinner

against firm fingers
now within the hole,
now a cavity,
your thumb started.

Your gray hand dips new water
to keep it pliable
and the rim takes an even finer tune
but you spot an imperfection,

with wire cut the spinning vase
down to a mixing bowl.

Another perfection check
reveals a new flaw
and the wire
reduces the clay to a cereal bowl.

Even that won't work
and the whole remaining lump bites the dust
in the recycling bin I'm astonished
how quickly destroyed, something so fine.

BLACK HOLE

Every now & then someone gets out of line
Here on Earth, and Mankind trembles:
Hitler treated Jews like ants
And some of us have relatives who died

In Vietnam, or Auschwitz, or just as needlessly
In some less public way.
How strange the names of places suggest ways to die!
It's like the flu, how that's never yet come from America!

Here on Earth we send out messages of love:
Space garbage, golf balls on the moon,
We say we hope the Martians land.
It'll help bring us more together.

Three

ONLY WHAT'S IMAGINED

Only what's imagined will not happen,
so I let myself worry about theft and
run-ins with the law. I can't elaborate,
it's too scary, but there's comfort having
thought it when you believe that very thought
wards off possibility. Extend the theory to
happy fantasies, the effect is devastating.
This can never happen to me now that I've thought it
pervades the moment from mounting the camel
with Gina Lollobridgida on the other side of the hump
to loping in tandem across the Sahara with cool
moments of lush and total isolation
at oases on the way. This can never happen
to me now as Gina drops from the camel
and loosens the halter. Her open mouth covers mine
as I try to chant "This can never happen,"
and she forces me backward into sand at the base
of lush grasses in soothing winds. The camel
looks the other way, politely fascinated
by the acres of sand he must cover beneath
the weight of our three months' provisions,
champagne and caviar for each oasis and a
few crab sandwiches for elevensies on the sand
to say nothing of a dozen sacks of dry camel feed.
Gina pants in my ear as I surrender
disbelief and feel her hand encircling, taking charge
and then she covers me with kisses
as, slowly, she peels back my robe.
I close my eyes then blink them rapidly,
up through the palms to a baked blue sky,
green slur in foreground, burning blue much higher,
farther from me than eyes in the air
blinking back their disappointment, disbelief.

THE TERRORISTS

We seized the President's family
and demanded this year's defense budget
be used to replace the ozone layers.
We used photographs of Margaret Thatcher with the Prince
to convince the British we meant business.
We circled the Kremlin with flagons of laughing gas
and got Gorbachev's detractors so silly
they realigned priorities and declared
complete cooperation with their friends
across the tiny sea and the continents
that had shrunk faster than the human brain
could grow.

Until now. We saw the chance to reverse the earth's destruction
and we leapt for it, billions of people saw through government
control or the control of other mortals.
None of us was pure. Even the Americans
had suffered intimidation at Kent State
and through their agencies and presidents.
We swore together, a billion voices,
we'd never lift arms when it wasn't
in our hearts to kill. That, alone,
ended most wars. Generals barked at empty barracks.

The President's wife became a regular Tanya Hearst,
screaming at the press that weapons never settled anything.
She really wowed them with that necklace of carbine shells
strung across her chest and the M-16 raised over her head.
It got so changed around from what you'd have expected
that I began to hope the pollution problem
would persist, bringing us to our senses
in this horrible way.

And I saw who were the terrorists.
Who'd manufactured the weapons we now carried,
who tried so hard to be big adults and grim,
at least in public, who made the styrofoam
and sold the refrigerators, the terrorists
in the supermarket spending their grocery money
for meats raised on carcinogens and wrapped
in tomorrow's solid waste problem.

I turned the bathroom mirror to the wall.
But like all the others I knew my silence would be the death
of any hope to have an earth to haunt,
at least an earth worth haunting
with people on it, say 100 years from now.
That's when I spoke. That's when we broke the ice.

Then all the world leaders, their international stress
so magically lifted, pardoned every one of us.
And we pardoned them.
It was a real love-in.
A bake-off of all that
crazy international tension. We sorted our trash.

And we shot canisters of ozone hundreds of miles up.
It was just like the 4th of July but much quieter.
No one needed to whoop it up in that sort of way.
And we all awoke with a warmth in our hearts
and we all started over. And the terror of peace
was known in many lands.

THEY'RE TELLING ME NOW

They're telling me now
a fine mist of gasoline, dispersed above the target
will cost no lives, create an electromagnetic pulse
that paralyzes the city below,
but there's no concussion, no fallout.

They're telling me now
a fine mist of gasoline, dispersed above the target
and then ignited by conventional flares, might create a pulse
that paralyzes the city below,
without concussion, no fallout.

And they're telling me now the enemy
will happily ignite the spigots of oil,
earth's blood we learned to pump —
the closest we could come to being hearts —
without concussion, no fallout

And that the smoke from their destruction
will block the earth's access to sunlight
long enough to threaten a nuclear winter:
there may be regions of the world
too dark and cold to sprout a small garden,
let alone survival crops.

They're telling me now
the world can't go on this way, we have to prevail
over human skullduggery no matter the price.
So we swim in our own blood
in battle for the earth's blood
and our thrashing makes us hearts.

We pump to keep it on the move,

to keep the helpless humans at our bidding
who will go to war when we want
to spoil the air they'll have to share
as we go down in history.

DABBLING IN OILS

words failing
I paint you a face like a kneecap
a scoop of heaven soft & firm support
it turns desire to energy
then back again.

To know you once more in that impossible house
only by painting I can ever see:
such patience it takes, such a drive's required
greater than dredging up words
to know foreground vs. background,
what should be the big thing in front
to give the rest perspective,
and where's the vanishing point Miss Cheek
tried to teach me about when I was in school,
too young to care?

Mixing colors slows me down
I back off & raise a thumb.
& not because I know what to do
I sight along the thumb, exhale
& move back in, it's time to sign

ink spilling from your doorway,
the shadow of an emptied house.

STEREOGRAM

I keep trying to lock you in
get my eyes to cross just so
the right image
merges with the left image
and the brain picks up a 3-D message.

To escape in lost focus!
As if looking at a picture long enough
will allow me to wander in,
look around, see the back side of things,
an ordinary schmuck made important with a stage pass
intent on befriending the star

and kind of hoping the world will notice.

It's like the many small hexagonal tiles
on bathroom floors in old hotels,
I love to watch my bare feet disappear
into the ages as, The Thinker, fist bracing chin,
elbow on knee, I study the universe
into which my toes can wiggle, pad around.

But — no! — you have to bend
or otherwise distort my vision,
close me out when I think I've locked you in,
an amateur with love songs to an image on the page,
who would have you know him, not just vice versa,
a picture responding to its viewer.
An art we haven't yet explored.

CHOCOLATAHOLIC, CHOCOHOLIC, CHOCO

Chocolate body paint! It makes me pant
to think of fingering up a glob to spread
across the landscape of your flesh,
the fragile part of you that shows
and tender parts that rarely see the light.

And if I buy a gallon of this stuff,
enough to cover you from head to toe,
you can be my Milky Way, my Mars Bar,
my M & M that melts in my hand and in my mouth.
You can be the sweet package of my youth,

a Necco Wafer held so long without a bite
saliva broke it down to sweet syrup
coating teeth and tongue and throat,
the dust I inhale, just molecules
broken from the basal cells and walking the air
until drawn in by a grabby nose.

So in your very presence I can take you in,
little bits of spirit and molecule
as well as all I've painted you to be,
my fingers are spoons and you can be
the plate from which my tongue lifts morsels.

PRECISION AIRLINES

From the little commuter plane,
Precision Airlines from
Montpelier to Boston,
I saw a whole nother side of things.

But first, how I feel about flying
with a line called "Precision."
It's the same way I felt about a company
that once tried to sell me a furnace,

"Reliable Heating" —
as if the name would compensate
for some grandiose flaw.
From Precision's plane I saw

how the roadways thread the forests and hills,
join up at the center of towns
and from there each sneaks
to a number of houses and farms,

past schoolyards with buses
lined up like pencils
and graveyards behind two identical
churches and behind the graveyards

a single junkyard, hidden on the ground, I'm sure
the juxtaposition confused by a comma
in the landscape, a strip of brush and scrub trees
but from the air, just a fencerow away.

MOMENTS ALONE

I emerge from a singing shower
naked as the piranha in my fish bowl
but for its scales
naked but for water as the water.

That fish bowl (really a tank)
sits in my bathroom
on a small table, by the toilet.
Why it's a piranha I'd as soon not go into.

Suffice to say it's a guard piranha,
not a pet. I tease him
at times while I'm taking a crap.
Cruelty to one's guards is how to keep 'em mean.

It's like the President, how he makes his look-alike,
the guy lucky enough to serve as a decoy
by coincidence of birth and the electorate's whim,
he's the only Secret Service agent doesn't have to stay in shape

unless the President is on a fitness kick
and decides to drop a hundred pounds,
makes his look-alike, in case of snipers,
emerge from the airplane first. "Go ahead,"

he says, giving his man a little, obnoxious push.
"They're cheering for you. Smile. Look happy.
Don't forget to wave."
Fresh from the shower

I wave into the mist on the mirror
as the piranha waves its tail, snarling at the glass.
The towel clears a path for my face
and if I stand on my toes, the entire body

gleams back, backwards:
my left foot is my right,
the knee I twitch comes back reversed.
I wonder who sees me and how.

2.

The eye has interest only
in what's not in the dark.
The finger touches only what has body
but being blind is startled when touched back.

It's a whole bowl full of surprises
for each of our senses! The ear
seeks color in sound but can't see it coming,
and so on for the whole five of them.

They pool their resources where the brain on its stem,
like a prodigy lollipop, runs the show
without any of the senses' skills,
depending on its runners, teenaged ganglia on their way up,

embittered veins and hardening arteries:
they were just born in the wrong place
hell, they could make a better decision
who gets off the plane,

when to exit the shower,
that piranha might be on the loose,
what songs to sing,
whether to shower or not.

DINOSAURS

A boy outgrows dinosaurs
and maybe always did feel, though awe, superior
if only because his family came later
"evolved higher," if you're willing to believe that stuff.
Although he does not yet know the word,
he treasures the irony that with humongous bodies
still in their skulls their brains were tiny
like the cockpits and their pilots up front and on top
of their giant 747's directing the future for 100,000 times
their weight, 230 lives and luggage other than their own.
And somewhere in the mansion developing in his brain,
his body grows to heroic proportions
with his capacity, self-doubt, to govern, at war in a land
he's learned to call feeling. By the time he's fifty
he'll be realizing he has a future and better start running
in spite of the collapse of his mansion, hell,
the entire estate, though body continues to grow.
Has there been a quarrel in the convent
or is he finally tuning in on compassion,
not just tolerance of his self,
bossy dreamer, but acceptance, *love?*
The corny stuff he's always known was there
but too big to control except by luck and faith.

MY WIFE WONDERS

how terrible it must have been
those 22 seconds when the commuter airplane
rolled out of control and flew full throttle
into earth. They must have known, she says,
they were going to die. Twenty-two seconds to ask
their final questions, say their final prayers.

Those are a long 22 seconds, she says,
that is not a quick death.
It must have been an eternity,
she muses, I don't like it.
And neither do I but you want it instant?
No time, no "eternity," no chance to reflect,
maybe even work up a laugh?

And remembers *her* airline "experience"
when on take-off a deer punctured a wheel
then got sucked into one of two jet engines
and the pilot came on the intercom
only after the plane was in the air and the cabin filling
with smoke, the smell of venison and electricity on fire:

"Aw folks, unfortunately, we've just struck a deer.
We're going to circle the airport, it won't hurt to burn up fuel,
and wait for ground to tell us if we have what it takes
to land this thing, I'll be back ... ."
And remembers the questions she heard as the ordeal extended:
"I wonder if anyone will know which kennel I left my dog at."

I could comment on the trivia
insisting itself forward at critical moments,

once you know you've bought the biscuit
as they say, seen the tomorrow cookies,
how my question might be
did anyone know I loved them?

Too general, too smooshy,
but the first that comes to mind.
Then, maybe, what should I wonder next?
I wonder if I'm wondering right,
savoring this final moment as I may
have savored birth, thinking if I thought at all,

through it all, I'm sure:
"Am I going to survive this?"

2.

I'm boarding a tiny commuter double prop
under someone else's name
and I'm scared: the digits in the flight number
add up to thirteen and I've always said
I'd never use someone else's ticket,
wouldn't change flight plans after the itinerary

was in from a travel agent,
I might volunteer to be bumped
off the one plane that did land safely.
And safe in my hotel room
it's too early to chortle,
I've got the return flight to encounter,

still using the round-trip tickets issued
to the guy who canceled his trip
at the last moment, in response to his wife's nightmare?
And all the thrill seekers can have their
midnight drives on western roads by moonlight
at ninety miles per hour with the headlights off.

I'll take 60 in full daylight on dry roads, no other
car in sight, four lanes, and *flat,*
let alone the roller coaster, it makes me puke
and I ain't into that, but I guess they all pale,
this virtual reality, this *eau d' eau*
or essence of essence compared to the whole, elongated trip.

No words can assess, no numbers quantify,
call it 22 seconds or 22 years,
it was there I almost remember spinning
out of control and flying full throttle
and didn't know I'd be glad
when it stopped.

DELICATE

It's delicate when we touch
each other, a careful mistake
will do but nothing more.
It's delicate the love
we carry and know
that only what waits
is separation
and let the new people
into your lives
or is this just a bunch
of hopeful crap?

It's delicate too this learning.
How even with degrees no one said
there'd be a *job*, but there is work
o there is work. How many
times I vacuum each week
is a measure of unemployment
though vacuuming is nothing I do for enjoyment.

I want me one of them *riding* vacuums,
metallic green with special bumpers
so I don't mar the furniture as I'm whizzing the room,
caroming off the pillars of our old upright piano
and making the long run down the hall,
wearing the safety helmet that came with the unit,
        wielding the magic wand
attachment at cobwebs as I glide by.

Cobwebs! Don't make me think of them.
Let me picture a spider's more symmetrical effort,
not the chaotic gathering of dust
in strands that hang from ceilings.
Let me think of spider webs,
the organization of desire,
a spider's fractal-like construction to ward off starvation,
a sticky, silver trampoline with "plenty of space to fly through,
just avoid the center!" claims the stupid moth
that fouls the whole web and isn't
anything the spider wants,
just a dusty pair of wings, fluttered to a mealy core,
the cobweb of the animal world.

Not to speak of the damaged web to rebuild
for, though resilient, a spider web is delicate
and delicate is like touch, like love, like learning,
like the finest, most expensive, tiniest chocolate
you're only supposed to have one of.

THE ULTIMATE COMMUTE

Every day, same time, he sees her car
on the two lane highway, approaching his car
as they drive to their jobs in opposite directions.
He memorizes her license plate,
he falls in love
with that sensuous face in the windshield
and those two, tenuous hands on the wheel,
always in the proper ten-til-two-o'clock position,
glimpsed each day
as they whistle past each other
to their work in opposite directions.

How can he meet her?
He lacks the courage to call her license number in
to Motor Vehicles and ask for her name,
address, home phone and marital status
or some details on the color of her eyes,
at forty miles per hour plus forty miles per hour
in the opposite direction, that's eighty miles per hour
at ten feet the closest they've ever been,
it's a miracle he even knows she's pretty,
or is he imagining that, too?
And willing?

So the complications are daunting.
The only reason he doesn't leave his job
is he'd miss this Mondays through Friday most weeks,
daily, instantaneous rendezvous,
no more than five seconds
from spotting her grill to seeing the tail lights
in the rearview mirror,

70

he's started to dread the weekends
because he knows she loves these meetings too.
Wasn't that a weak smile she managed
and a tentative wave of the fingertips,

a moment of danger when one hand
nearly left the wheel in a hot flash,
tempestuous, impetuous, and
for that moment vulnerable I'm sure?
The whole expression was Be My Friend
but in her embarrassment she missed
his reciprocation the next day and the next:
he carried a yellow rose by the stem
between his teeth, thorns sometimes spiking
the roof of his mouth and one day at work
he nursed a pierced lip.

He knows that on the hottest days of all,
when his trousers are thin and the top is down,
she's probably wearing a short skirt
and rubs herself as he does, suggestively,
each out of sight of the other, maybe
just a sentimental and funny reminder,
maybe in lust lost on the highway
each day where it begins,
that little pep talk you can give yourself
and with all your aging confidence you know
she's giving herself too.

JUST KIDDING, HONEST

Your young son's young friend,
the one whose successful brain surgery
removed not all speech but, strangely,
his nouns: it turns out they'd also been stored
on the other side of his brain,
he just had to find them
and the access key was music,
all the TV and radio jingles starting with
Chicquita Banana and I'm Here to Say:
makes me more aware than ever
it's a fucking computer we carry
between our ears, these audio terminals,
and when I saw the special
on brain surgery I learned they pin little numbers
to the lobes where certain impulses register. Honest.

I guess everyone's wired a little different
so a naked nurse passes through intensive care
your hard-on tells 'em you noticed
and a 26 is pinned to the point in your brain
where the pulsing soon makes wisps of smoke
that sting the surgeons' eyes behind their masks
and the one with the good bedside manner makes a crack
how he now knows where to cut
if you ever wave that big dong at his wife. Just kidding.

It's a crude part of mine they'd want to pin down
and eliminate, cynical distrust and a laugh
that echoes from hemisphere to hemisphere,
here I am! here I am!

as, desperate for a target, in a pulse,
just kidding, honest, for a laugh,
the red-eyed, red-faced surgeons swipe their scalpels
or probe nouns and music with a swab
to rescue language, hoping for the truth.

-for Ellen

THE LAST WORDS

Oh Heavens! Such a
tiny airplane & the pilot's
a whacky straight who got his training free
during Vietnam.

Something unfortunate occurs with an aileron
I don't understand but it means curtains
and all we can do is fly around as low as possible
until the gas runs out.

The winds toss us considerably and the radio says
we're too far off course, of course, to pinpoint, we'll have
to chance it, crash land in the darkness on the mountainside
when the final spiral

down begins.
There. It is fairly clear we are going to die.
I turn to the pilot
and tell him how wonderful he's been

how he's been the most important bullshit
in my life I am not thinking to speak of you

oh God